D1508494

the
101
BEST
GRAPHIC
NOVELS

For my father, 1915-1998

the 101 BEST GRAPHIC NOVELS

by Stephen Weiner

Edited by
Keith R.A. DeCandido

NANTIER · BEALL · MINOUSTCHINE
Publishing inc.
new york

We have over 150 graphic
novels in stock. Ask for our
complete color catalog:
NBM publishing
555 8th Ave. Suite 1202
New York, NY 10018

See our website and go to our Library
page for recommendations
www.nbmpublishing.com

Some of the entries in the bibliography
first appeared in a similar form in
"Library Journal".

ISBN 1-56163-283-X hardcover
ISBN 1-56163-284-8 paperback
ISBN 1-56163-285-6 library edition
covers © their respective owners
© 2001 Stephen Weiner
Printed in Hong Kong

5   4   3   2   1

Library of Congress Cataloging-in-Publication Data

Weiner, Stephen, 1955-
    The 101 best graphic novels / by Stephen Weiner; edited by Keith DeCandido.
       p. cm.
    Includes bibliographical references and index.
       ISBN 1-56163-283-X (alk. paper) -- ISBN 1-56163-284-8 (pbk. : alk. paper)
       1. Graphic novels--Bibliography. I. Title: One hundred one best graphic novels. II.
DeCandido, Keith R. A. III. Title.

    Z5956.C6 W45 2001
    [PN6710]
    016.7415'9--dc21

                                                                        2001030622

Acknowledgements

For their help with this book, I'd like to thank the following people:

Neil Gaiman for his contribution; Tony Davis and Tom Devlin, for their advice, research, and help; Keith R.A. DeCandido, for a fine editing job; and Terry Nantier, for taking on this project. I'd also like to thank Rachel, Julian, and Lily, for everything.

Stephen **Weiner** is a leading specialist in building graphic novel collections in public libraries which are embracing the form enthusiastically. He has published articles, reviews and poetry, and is the author of *Bring an Author to Your Library* as well as *50 Community Service Projects for Teens* (with Senator Edward Kennedy). He is the director of the Maynard Public Library in Maynard, MA, and holds a M.A. in Children's Literature.

Editor **Keith R.A. DeCandido** is a best-selling author of assorted novels, comic books, eBooks, short stories, and nonfiction books in the science fiction and fantasy media fields. A former comics journalist for Library Journal, Publishers Weekly, Wilson Library Bulletin, Creem, and The Comics Journal, he has also edited over fifty books based on comic book characters (and written a few). Learn more about him on the web at DeCandido.net.

Table of Contents

Author's Preface   9

A Very Short History of Comics and Graphic Novels   11

The 101 Best Graphic Novels   17

Novels Featuring Comic Book Characters   59

Further Reading About and Related to Comics   67

Index   75

Author's Preface

In 1965, I received eight well-read comic books as Christmas presents, and my future was assured. During the next several years, I followed the exploits of Spider-Man, Daredevil, and Thor, to the point where I recited dialogue from their stories as my friends and I wrestled. I became so involved in the comic book mythos that I wrote a high school term paper on "Comic Books as Literature," and later taught a high-school-level course on the history of American comic books.

By the mid-1970s, the artwork and ingenuity that had made comic books so compelling began to lose its grip, and when I sold my collection to supplement my college education, I wasn't sure I'd ever look back. And I didn't; for ten years I read novels, Greek drama, and poetry and entered the teaching profession. And as a teacher, in search of material for my students, I entered the same comic book store I'd last set foot in a decade before. While scanning the racks for good stuff I discovered that the playing field had changed; superheroes still dominated the field, but there were other, more probing pieces as well, called graphic novels. I soon found myself researching the graphic novel field as much for my own interest as for potential reading matter for my students.

I also saw an industry turning upon itself and growing inward. Because of the comic book store venue, publishers were able to produce works aimed solely at a particular clientele: comic book readers. Because I was older, yet still interested in reading superhero stories, I was attracted to the more mature and literate stories.

In 1987, I left teaching and entered the library profession. As a graduate student, I wrote papers defending the place of Art Spiegelman's *Maus* in the library, as well as studies of heroism in the work of Jack Kirby. As a working librarian, I struggled to include graphic novels in the library's collection, and as one result of including comic book materials, circulation increased and the public library, as an institution, swaggered just a bit from a hip appeal.

In 1995, I returned to teaching. This time the classroom was my house, and the student was my son, who was learning to read. It wasn't easy at first; he had difficulty making the connection between the words he'd heard read and those on the printed page. Then we tried comics, which made a bridge between words and ideas, pictures and stories. In the course of one academic year, from reading comic books, he moved up two grade levels in reading level and comprehension. Within two years following that, he was reading graphic novels and prose novels indiscriminately.

I have two hopes for those of you who hold this book in your hands: that you will, as I did, take the leap into the wild and wonderful world of graphic novels, and that you use the medium for your own purpose. If you are a parent, explore the possibility of reading graphic novels with your children. If you are a book reader, search out those graphic novels that will hold your attention. If you are a teacher, bookstore owner, or librarian, use graphic novels professionally. The medium has boundless potential as an educational tool and an American art form.

A Very Short History of Comics and Graphic Novels

Comics historians might argue that the first comics were cave paintings depicting battles and tribal rituals, but American comics began in 1895, with the publication of the first newspaper strip, The *Yellow Kid* by R.F. Outcault. The comic strip form caught the attention of the reading public and, as a result, the comic strip became very popular in the early part of this century. Sunday and daily comic strips continue to be featured in almost every newspaper in the United States.

Comic books didn't become popular until the 1930s, and were initially reprints of newspaper strips. However, with the growing popularity of pulp fiction, publishers were looking for new ways to compete in the market. Soon, original stories started appearing in comic book periodicals that previously only reprinted strips. For many people who observe the field peripherally, the 1930s remain the defining moment of comic book history: many of the superheroes who remain popular today were created in the years just prior to World War II.

As a genre, comic books mirrored popular culture. Comic books in the early 1940s had a distinctly patriotic flavor—indeed, many were straight-out Allied propaganda. Those in the 1950s had a more conservative tone—it was in this decade that the romance and Western comics flourished. Coexisting with those, however, was a radical strain—the EC horror, crime, and science fiction comics. The 1950s were also the period when the comic book field came under attack as deleterious to the morals of American youth. Dr. Frederic Wertham's book, *The Seduction of the Innocent*, blamed juvenile delinquency on the effect of comic books. Worried, comic book publishers, created the Comics Code Authority (CCA), which created guidelines for acceptable and unacceptable content. EC dropped its radical comics rather than adopt the CCA's rules, and turned *Mad* magazine into a newsstand periodical not bound by the new regulations. Romances and Westerns flourished.

Superhero comics returned in the late 1950s and flourished in the 1960s. As America had become a more introspective society, the

13

new superheroes, embodied by Spider-Man, were imbued with phobias and challenges. The 1960s also witnessed the emergence of underground comix, which expressed discontent with middle-American values. Superhero and other mainstream comic books were sold in drugstores and newsstands; underground comix couldn't be sold there because they were not approved by the CCA. Instead, they were sold where their intended audience shopped: head shops. This was the first time anyone in the comics field attempted to niche market; previously, comic book publishers had attempted to sell to the largest audience possible, but the underground comix' success proved that one could make a profit by appealing directly to readers with a similar political ideal or artistic aesthetic as the comics' creators.

In the early 1970s, the comic book convention was initiated, allowing comic book dealers direct access to collectors. The comic book industry was beginning to turn inside. At conventions, rare and prized comic books were sold at collector's prices. Soon, the comic book specialty shop was pioneered: a place where underground comix and mainstream comics found common ground, perhaps because both strains of popular culture existed outside the mainstream. As a concept, the comic book specialty shop thrived in part because the forum allowed publishers direct contact with their readership. As a result, many publishers experimented with different kinds of books, directed at different segments of the comic book store patronage.

Other factors were important as well. Comic book creators in the United States were utilizing cartooning methods developed by Japanese and European creators, bringing a new sophistication into American comic books. Underground comix moved closer to the mainstream and used accepted comic book characters to examine attitudes and beliefs previously left unexplored by more conventional comic book creators.

In the 1980s, superheroes became societal outcasts, burdened with complex personalities and problems. These were stories not meant for ten-year-olds, but ten-year-olds who had matured but still liked reading comics. Artwork became more expressive and storylines increasingly demanding. Comic books featuring heroes that weren't so super grew more intricate and literary than they had been previously. Comic book readers had to grow more literate to comprehend the involved storylines. Ironically, comics became more literate at the same time that national reading scores began to decline.

The graphic novel grew out of experimentation in the comic book field in the late 1970s and early 1980s, and attempted to create a sophisticated story, told in comic book format, in one full-length book. The form became popular with readers who tired of visiting their favorite (or any!) comic book shop only to find that the next issue of the storyline they were interested in was unavailable. By the end of the 1980s, several publishers ceased producing serials, and concentrated their efforts solely on graphic novels. It also proved a handy format for collecting self-contained stories that ran over several issues.

Now, over a century after *The Yellow Kid*, the graphic novel comes in many forms: the strip collection that started it all is still going strong, as are reprints of other serialized stories, with original works still being published ranging from the historical to the biographical, and from high adventure to low comedy.

And who knows what this new century might bring?

The 101
Best Graphic
Novels

Narrowing the tremendous field of choices to 101 was difficult enough—to rank them within that would be impossible. Therefore the following list is in the indiscrimate form of alphabetical by creator(s). Each entry is also given an indicator as to reading level: C for all ages; Y for all ages above 12; A: adults, too complex for children. **Note well that these choices were made based on what is currently in print and available!**

Allred, Michael. **Madman: The Oddity Odyssey.**
Acacia Press, 1999, $14.95, ISBN 087816314X, **C**
Madman is a charmingly goofy hero in the tradition of the 1960s Batman television series rather than the brutally realistic Batman movies of the 1980s and 1990s. This first book of his adventures finds Madman at the clutches of his arch enemy, Mr. Monstadt, fighting for the secret journals of Dr. Boiffard!

Aragones, Sergio & Mark Evanier. **Groo & Rufferto.**
Dark Horse, 2000, $9.95, ISBN 1569714479, **C**
This spoof of the barbarian comic popularized by Marvel's *Conan* comics

of the 1970s features the helpless, hap-less, and hopeless barbarian Groo. Aragones honed his craft as an artist at *MAD* magazine, and his skill is consummate and his product hilarious. Other titles include *Groo: The Most Intelligent Man in the World, The Groo Bazaar, The Groo Houndbook, The Groo Inferno,* and *The Life of Groo.*

Bagge, Peter. **Hey Buddy! Volume 1 of the Complete Buddy Bradley Stories from** *Hate.*
Fantagraphics Books, 1995, $12.95, ISBN 1560971134, **A**

Hate is Peter Bagge's ode to those who live on the edge, whose world consists of comic book shops, used record and book stores, and whose idea of horror is holding a job requiring some responsibility. Hey Buddy! is an engaging look at peripheral people who exist primarily for the next issue, next CD, or next book sale. One can sense the influence of Robert Crumb in these black-and-white illustrations.

Baker, Kyle. **Why I Hate Saturn**.
DC Comics, 1998 (reprint of 1990 edition), $17.95, ISBN 0930289722, **Y**

Annie and Ricky are fringe players, who eke out a living as columnists for Daddy-O, a magazine appealing to the the hip and disenfranchised. When Annie's crazy sister suddenly reappears, Annie is forced to make a commitment to someone other than herself. In doing so, she willingly puts herself in danger and confronts the U.S. military. Why I Hate Saturn is saturated with irreverance and tongue-in-cheek humor.

Bechdel, Alison. **Dykes to Watch Out For.**
Firebrand Books, 1995, $8.95, ISBN 0932379176, **A**
This early novella of lesbian friends and lovers Clarice, Toni, Lois, and Mo are funny, insightful, and heartbreaking. The universality of the characters and the situations makes this book of interest to anyone intrigued by romantic trauma and career dilemmas. Other titles include *Dykes to Watch Out For: The Sequel; Hot Throbbing Dykes to Watch Out For; More Dykes to Watch Out For, New Improved! Dykes to Watch Out For, Post-Dykes to Watch Out For; Spawn of Dykes to Watch Out For,* and *Split-Level Dykes to Watch Out For.*

Bendis, Brian Michael. **Fortune and Glory**.
Oni Press, 2000, $14.95, ISBN 1929998066, **Y**
This book is a "journal" in comics form of successful comic book writer Bendis's experiences while trying to break into the world of Hollywood screen writing. A good choice for non-comic book readers, and a biting look at the movie industry.

Brabner, Joyce, Harvey Pekar & Frank Stack. **Our Cancer Year.**
Four Walls, Eight Windows, 1994, $17.95, ISBN 1568580118, **A**
This account of Pekar's battle with cancer as told by him and his coauthor/wife Brabner is illustrated with compassion by Frank Stack. The result is a gut-wrenching reading experience.

Briggs, Raymond. **Ethel & Ernest**.
Jonathan Cape, 1998, $21.00, ISBN 0224046624, **Y**.
Briggs is possibly the premier cartoonist publishing exclusively with major publishing houses, and any new work of his deserves a very careful reading. Here, we are presented with a story for adults, the cartoon version of Briggs' parents lives. What comes across is a social history of Britain from the years prior to the Second World War to the death of both Briggs' parents in 1971, as his parents lives and his own are caught within larger political events.

Briggs, Raymond. **The Snowman.**
Random House, 1995 (reprint of 1978 edition), $3.99, ISBN 0679872736, **C**
This magical adventure of a boy and his snowman teaches children about various stages of life. Told wordlessly, readers follow nameless characters on a journey through life to death.

Brown, Chester. **I Never Liked You.**
Drawn & Quarterly, 1994, $12.95, ISBN 0969670168, **A**
Brown's biting commentary on adolescent insecurity and search for love is moving and true to life. The book design is particularly effective in conveying teen isolation and yearning. Clearly, this is one of best graphic novels articulating a realistic coming of age. For readers who read (and re-read) J.D. Salinger's *The Catcher in the Rye*.

Burns, Charles. **Big Baby.**
Fantagraphics Books, 1999, $24.95, ISBN 1560973617, **A**
Tony's overactive imagination is stimulated by television and comic books, but somehow his imaginary world clarifies the real world as the two intersect in each of these 4 stories. Exquisitely rendered in black and white, these stories both parody and articulate the repressive culture of 1950's America. Also of interest: EL BORBAH(Fantagraphics).

Busiek, Kurt & Brent Anderson. **Kurt Busiek's Astro City: Life in the Big City.**
DC Comics, 2000 (reprint of 1996 edition), $19.95,
ISBN 156389551X, **Y**
This tribute to golden age superhero lore is a charmer. Busiek plays both raconteur and historian in this collection of volumes from the serial, as he aptly tells a variety of tales about the heroes of Astro City, from the Samaritan, who quests for a normal life but is prevented from it by world-saving and crime fighting, to a lowly thug who accidentally discovers Jack-in-the-Box's secret identity, a revelation that does *not* bring him the good fortune he expects. Anderson's illustrations are slow and musing, providing a good vehicle for these stories. Other titles include *Family Album* and *Confessions*.

Busiek, Kurt & Alex Ross. **Marvels.**
Marvel Entertainment Group, 1994,
$19.95, ISBN 0785100490, **Y**
Throughout the history of superhero
comics, the newspaper profession has
played a pivotal role. The secret identi-
ties of both Superman and Spider-Man
are journalists. The protagonist of
Marvels is a photographer who has no
other identity, but tries to document how
normal people feel as they walk among
the super-powered. *Marvels* probably res-
onates more strongly with readers famil-
iar with the Marvel superhero universe,
but is still a very compelling look at the normal-person's view of a super-
world.

Byrne, John. **Man of Steel.**
DC Comics, 1988, $7.50,
ISBN 0930289285, **C**
In an effort to update and revitalize their
superhero line, DC assigned Byrne the
task of retelling and updating Superman's
origin and early years. This revision
became the standard for the character—it
was even followed in ABC's *Lois & Clark*
TV series and the WB's animated
Superman TV series. The kids will like it,
and adults should be entertained.

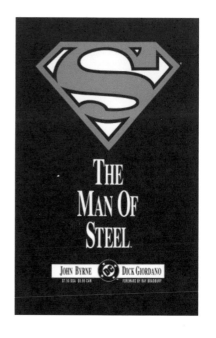

Chandler, Raymond & Michael Lark.
**Raymond Chandler's Philip Marlowe:
My Little Sister.**
Fireside Books, 1997, $15.00, ISBN 0684829339, **Y**

Chandler's work has been transposed into films, but this is the first attempt to tell a Chandler story in the comics format, in this remake of the 1949 mystery novel, The Little Sister. Large chunks of Chandler's original text compliment Lark's able adaptation, giving the book an eerie, 1930s cinematic texture.

Clowes, Daniel. **Ghostworld.**
Fantagraphic Books, 1997, $9.95, ISBN 1560972998, **A**
Enid and Becky are codependent friends as high school ends. However, Enid's vague desire to attend college drives them apart, and Becky develops a relationship with Josh, whom Enid also admires. Becky's relationship with Josh helps distance her from Enid. Enid's efforts to overcome her jealousy and her decision at the book's resolution is shattering and surprising, as true revelations are in all fiction, and readers are left to ponder how life decisions are made. Beautifully illustrated.

Crumb, Robert. **The Complete Crumb Comics: The Death of Fritz the Cat.**
Fantagraphics Books, 1992, $39.95, ISBN 1560970774, **A**
Crumb is perhaps the genius of the underground comix movement in the 1960s and one of the great American artists of this century. In this, the eighth of over a dozen volumes collecting all of Crumb's varied work over the decades, we get to see Fritz the Cat killed—a rather extreme reaction to Crumb's disgust for the animated movie treatment of his creation by Ralph Bakshi.

Cruse, Howard. **Stuck Rubber Baby.**
DC Comics, 1995, $24.95, ISBN 1563892162, $14.95 pb, ISBN

1563892553, **Y**

This 1960s-era coming of age novel is the journey of a gay white man in the South struggling for a personal and sexual identity. Readers experience the conflict inherent in Toland's search for personal meaning as well as the murder of a close friend. Told with evocative, atmospheric illustrations, Cruse weaves a tale that stretches over a twenty-year period. *Stuck Rubber Baby* is an especially good choice for readers uninterested in genre graphic novels.

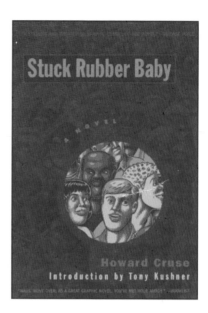

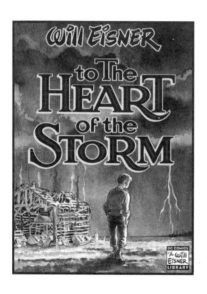

Eisner, Will. **A Contract with God and Other Tenement Stories.**
DC Comics, 2000 (reprint of 1978 edition), $12.95, ISBN 1563896745, **Y**
Eisner, Will. **To The Heart of The Storm.**
DC Comics, 2000, $14.95,
ISBN 1563896796, **Y**
Eisner, Will. **Minor Miracles**.
DC Comics, 2000, $12.95
ISBN 1563897555, **Y**

Contract contains four interrelated coming-of-age stories set in a Bronx tenement in the 1930s. This was one of the early experiments with the graphic novel format as a vehicle for telling an original, self-contained story. Also by Eisner—who may well be the comic field's Henry Roth (*Call It Sleep*)—is *To the Heart of the Storm* an autiobiographical novel about a cartoonist's anti-Semitic experienes prior to World War II. *Minor Miracles*, his latest endeavor, consists of 4 short stories relating events that affect a family, a group, or city block, and are direct tales of individual survival

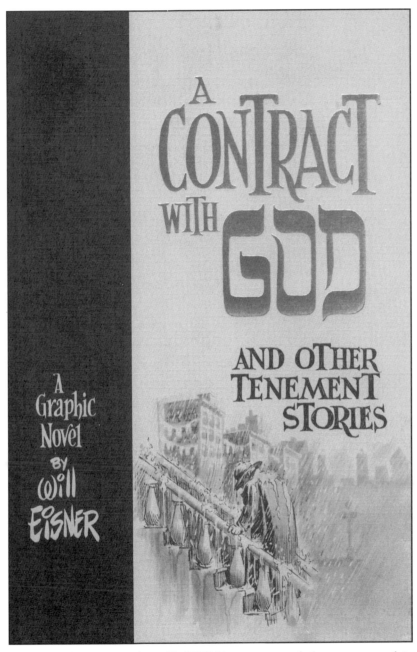

The one that started it all: Will Eisner coined the term **graphic novel** while pitching *A Contract With God* to general trade publishers. Above is the cover of the first edition from Baronet Publishing, 1978.

often dependent on the unexpected generosity of others. The fact that people care enough about each other to insure survival is the miracle Eisner tells of. Survival comes in many forms: financial generosity, cleverness, invisibility, and forgiveness. Eisner's illustration and narrative style are direct. The book is completely black and white, and the drawings convey subtle actions without adornment.

Eisner, Will. **The Spirit Archives. Volume 1.**
DC Comics, 2000, $49.95,
ISBN 1563896737, **C**

This reprints the first six months of the immensely popular and influential strip by Eisner. Lawman Denny Colt put on a mask and called himself the Spirit in order to fight crime. Although a simple adventure comic on the face of it, *The Spirit* revolutionized sequential art storytelling.

Feiffer, Jules. **Meanwhile...**
HarperCollins, 1999 (reprint of 1997 edition), $5.95,
ISBN 0062059335, **C**
When hyperactive Raymond is bored with one situation, he "meanwhiles" to another, landing climactically inside each adventure. Feiffer plays quite successfully with the comic book convention "meanwhile," a method of keeping the action moving from frame to frame.

Feiffer, Jules. **Tantrum!**
Fantagraphics Books, 1997 (reprint of 1979 edition), $16.95, ISBN 1560972823, **A**
This drama of midlife crisis is as com-

pelling today as when it first appeared. Protagonist Leo asks: What is the value of growing older? As a reaction to middle age, Leo reverts to babyhood. However, with the wisdom of years, can childhood remain innocent? The "splash and scratch" drawings move the narrative forward with almost mindless speed.

Friedman, Michael Jan, Peter David, & Pablo Marcos. **Star Trek: The Modala Imperative.**
DC Comics, 1992, $19.95, ISBN 1563890402, **C**

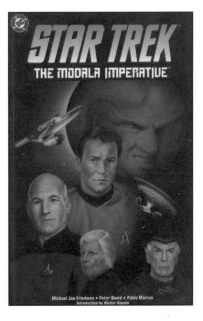

Star Trek is immensely popular in whatever form it appears, as a television show, a novel, or a graphic novel. This story spans both *Star Trek* and *The Next Generation*, as Friedman chronicles a mission of Captain Kirk's that has to be finished a century later by Captain Picard in an adventure written by David, with the characters of Spock and McCoy appearing in both. This book should keep *Star Trek* and general science fiction fans satisfied. Other *Trek* volumes of note include *Debt of Honor, False Colors, The Mirror Universe,* and *Who Killed Captain Kirk?*

Gaiman, Neil, et al. **The Books of Magic.**
DC Comics, 1993, $19.95, ISBN 1563890828, **Y**
In a story reminiscent of the British fantasists Alan Garner and Susan Cooper, young Tim Hunter reluctantly joins a magic circle that he will someday rule. Arthurian fantasy doesn't translate into the graphic novel medium better than this.

Gaiman, Neil, et al. **The Sandman: The Doll's House.**
DC Comics, 1990, $19.95, ISBN 0930289595, **A**

Gaiman's *The Sandman* monthly series was a reinvention of a minor 1940's hero, and Gaiman drew extensively on world mythologies, binding storylines of fragile humans and deities older than gods to create a seamless tapestry upon which compelling stories are told. Sandman was mainstream comics' most serious attempt to create a new mythology for adults, and this particular story, *The Doll's House*, articulates Gaiman's answer as to why gods exist. Other titles include *Brief Lives*, *Dream Country*, *The Dream Hunters*, *Fables and Reflections*, *A Game of You*, *The Kindly Ones*, *Preludes and Nocturnes*, *Season of Mists*, *The Wake*, and *World's End*.

Gaiman, Neil & Dave McKean. **Mr. Punch.**
DC Comics, 1994, $17.95, ISBN 1563892464, **Y**
Gaiman, Neil & Dave McKean. **Violent Cases.**
Kitchen Sink Press, 1998, (reprint of 1987 edition). $12.95, ISBN 0878165576, **Y**
Writer Gaiman and artist McKean team for these two very different tales. *Mr. Punch* is a chilly contemporary version of the medival "Punch and Judy" play, which is painted in watercolor, and steeped in mythology, folklore, and literature. *Violent Cases* begins as a mystery/gangster story, but it evolves into a study of memory and desire, and readers are chilled by the ironic conclusion. McKean's art is sure and narrative, and the characters are distinct while remaining distant. Take your hat off while you read this one.

Geary, Rick. **The Borden Tragedy: A Memoir of the Infamous Double Murder at Fall River, Mass., 1892.**

NBM ComicsLit, 1997, $8.95,
ISBN 1561631892, **Y**

Geary, Rick. **Jack the Ripper: A Journal of the Whitechapel Murders 1888-1889.**
NBM ComicsLit, 1995, $15.95,
ISBN 1561631248, **Y**

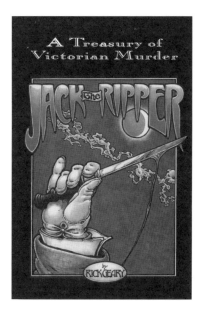

These two little books are part of Geary's "Treasury of Victorian Murder" series. *The Borden Tragedy* presents a restrained account of the infamous double slaying, as told by an anonymous observer close to the Borden family. Readers sympathize with the public smearing of Lisbeth "Lizzie" Borden, and are relieved at the trial's outcome. Geary wryly notes the similarities between the Borden trial of the 1890s and the O.J. Simpson trial of the 1990s. In *Jack the Ripper*, Geary turns an impartial and clear eye on the horrific crimes committed against prostitutes in Whitechapel. The illustrations are poignant, unsentimental, and move the narratives along handily. Both volumes include a bibliography. (See also Alan Moore & Eddie Campbell's *From Hell*.)

Giardino, Vittorio. **A Jew in Communist Prague, Volume 1: Loss of Innocence.**
NBM ComicsLit, 1997, $11.95, ISBN 1561631809, **A**
This first book in the series recounts the childhood of Jonas Finkel, whose father is mysteriously taken by the police in 1950 communist Prague. Young Finkel is victimized by anti-Semitism, removed from school, forced to work as an errand boy, and isolated from his peers. The story ends hopefully as Jonas and his mother learn that his father is alive and held in a prison camp. Told in clear, understated illustrations, and colored primarily with greens and blues, this graphic novel offers a touch of Kafka while being gentle on the eyes. Volumes 2 and 3 are also presently available in this quartet-to-be.

Gonick, Larry. **Larry Gonick's The Cartoon History of the Universe.**
William Morrow, 1982, $11.00, ISBN 0688010113, **Y**

One of the most popular, widely read and reviewed books in the graphic novel format, this book provides clear historical information using a visual orientation and a humorous approach.

Goodwin, Archie & Al Williamson. **Classic** *Star Wars*.
Dark Horse, 1995 (reprint of 1990 edition), $16.95, ISBN 1569711097, **Y**
Goodwin's facile scripts and Williamson's cinematic art retell and expand on the *Star Wars* movie themes in this collection of the first *Star Wars* newspaper strips published from 1981-1984.

The Greatest Joker Stories Ever Told.
DC Comics, 1989, $14.95, ISBN 0930289366, **C**
The Greatest Superman Stories Ever Told.
DC Comics, 1987, $15.95, ISBN 0930289390, **C**
The Greatest Team-Up Stories Ever Told.
DC Comics, 1991, $14.95, ISBN 0930289617, **C**
These volumes collect stories from over five decades' of comics history, including various interpretations of Batman's arch-enemy, the Joker; a wide range of Superman stories, from the simplistic to the self-doubting; and some fine examples of heroes working together, the best of which is a surprising Superman/Swamp Thing pairing.

Griffith, Bill, **Zippy Annual #1**.
Fantagraphic Books, 2000, $19.95, ISBN 156097351X, **Y**
Social commentators Griffy(Griffith) and his alter-ego Zippy are apt and incisive. This book collects numerous episodes from the daily Zippy news-

paper strip. Griffith has also created a full length Zippy graphic novel, *Are We Having Fun Yet?* (Fantagraphic Books). Other Zippy collections include *Pointed Behavior, Zippy Stories, and Pindemonium.*

Groening, Matt, et al. **Simpsons Comics a Go-Go.**
HarperPerennial, 2000, $11.95, ISBN 006095566X, **C**
The Simpsons TV series has made a tremendous impact on our culture, so it's no surprise that they also have their own comic book, which retains the scathing wit of its source. This collects several issues of the monthly serial and will delight any *Simpsons* viewer. Other titles include *Simpsons Comics Big Bonanza, Simpsons Comics Extravaganza, Simpsons Comics Simps-O-Rama, Simpsons Comics Strike Back,* and *Simpsons Comics Wingding.*

Hergé. **Tintin in Tibet.**
Little, Brown, 1988 (reprint of 1975 edn.), $9.95, ISBN 0316358398, **C**
Tintin and his dog Snowy have enchanted readers from all over the world. In this installment, the boy reporter and his dog travel to exotic Tibet. The drawings are expressive and clear, and Herge's sense of story masterful.

Hernandez, Gilbert. **Love & Rockets: Poison River.**
Fantagraphics Books, 1994, $16.95, ISBN 1560971517, **A**
Whether it in the comic book or graphic novel formats, *Love & Rockets*, created by brothers Gilbert and Jaime Hernandez, was one of the most respected and supported adult alternative comics. The characters in most of Gilbert's stories live on the fringe society in the Mexican town of Palomar. *Poison River* centers around the long and confusing love affair between Peter and Lubita.

Other volumes of note are *Blood of Palomar* and *Duck Feet* by Gilbert; *Chester Square*, *The Death of Speedy*, and *Wigwam Bam* by Jaime; and *Chelo's Burden*, *House of Raging Women*, *Las Mujeres Perdidas*, and *Music for Mechanics* by both.

Jackson, Jack. **Lost Cause: The True Story of Famed Texas Gunslinger John Wesley Hardin.**
Kitchen Sink Press, 1998, $16.95, ISBN 0878166181, **Y**

This well-researched docudrama tells the story of Texas's struggle for law and order, particularly from the pre-Civil War years into the reconstruction era.
Writer/artist/historian Jackson sees gunfighter and outlaw John Wesley Hardin as the symbol of Texas's struggle—first as an outlaw, then as a citizen hoping for redemption. The illustrative style resembles movie stills, reinforcing the documentary approach. Essential reading.

Johnston, Lynn. **A Look Inside...For Better or For Worse: The Tenth Anniversary Collection.**
Andrews & McMeel, 1989, $12.95, ISBN 0836218531, **C**
This strip focuses on warm tales of family life, and finds humor and emotion in the interactions among the different generations. One of the best family-centered newspaper strips.

Kafka, Franz & Peter Kuper. **Give It Up! and Other Stories by Franz Kafka.**
NBM ComicsLit, 1995, $15.95, ISBN 1561631256, **A**
In the introduction to this book, Jules Feiffer aptly compares these studies of Kafka's stories with a woodcut look to jazz versions of Gershwin

compositions. Kafka's sense of alienation is very real in Kuper's chilling and poignant art, which is interpretive rather than merely graphic. (See also David Mairowitz & Robert Crumb's *Introducing Kafka*.)

Kanan, Nabiel. **Lost Girl.**
NBM ComicsLit, 1999, $9.95, ISBN 1561632295, **Y**
On vacation with her family, teenage Beth is drawn to a "wild girl", a young woman who scorns societal norms, and appears happily homeless. Beth is increasingly drawn to the wild girl's rebellious lifestyle, which seems a true expression of individuality. However, when Beth suspects that her friend holds a young girl hostage, she attempts to free herself from the wild girl's hypnotic influence. After she returns home, the routine of getting ready to return to school disappoints Beth, and she feels the influence of the wild girl so strongly that she must act. The black and white drawings accurately reflect the story's understated, seductive quality.

Katchor, Ben. **Julius Knipl, Real Estate Photographer: Stories.**
Little Brown, 1996, $12.95, ISBN 0316482943, **Y**
Photographer Julius Knipl takes to the streets in a city much like Manhattan, only to discover its residents lost in a nostalgic dream of what never

was. The dialogue is crisp and confident, and the drawings border both realistic and dreamlike. Readers may also enjoy an earlier Knipl volume, *Cheap Novelties: The Pleasures of Urban Decay* (Little Brown, 1991).

Keaton, Russell. **The Aviation Art of Russell Keaton.**
Kitchen Sink Press, 1995, $24.95, ISBN 0878163883, **C**
This is the only collection of comic strip *Flyin' Jenny*, the only comic about a female aviator, and the first strip to feature a professional woman.

These high-flying adventures feature strong feminist themes.

Kelly, Walt. **Pogo. Volume 11.**
Fantagraphics Books, 2000, $9.95,
ISBN 1560973390, **C**
Kelly's supreme political commentary, presented as a newspaper
comic strip, remains a high point
in comic strip art. Fantagraphics
has been presenting *Pogo* in its
entirety in this multi-volume
series.

Kelso, Megan. **Queen of the Black Black.**
Highwater Books, 1998, $12.95, ISBN 096656304, **A**
Kelso's bittersweet, poignant stories of early adulthood range from temp
work, unwanted pregnancies, to decisions about the best way to have an
extramarital affair. The black and white drawings are expressive and
pointed.

Kipling, Rudyard & P. Craig Russell.
Rudyard Kipling's Jungle Book.
NBM, 1997, $16.95,
ISBN 1561631523, **C**
Russell's brilliant and affecting adaptation of Kipling's story of wild man
Mowgli, who preceded Burroughs'
Tarzan, and is a more realized and finite
character, is presented here in illustrations that come alive and soothe the
eyes. Readers feel what it is to be part of
the pack, the thrill of the hunt, and the
many ways that humanity threatens
wildlife. As the story concludes, we are

moved by Mowgli's ultimate choice. This is one of several fine comics adaptations of classic works by Russell.

Kirby, Jack. **Jack Kirby's New Gods.**
DC Comics, 1998, $11.95, ISBN 1563893851, **C**
Kirby was the explosive force behind the superhero revival in the 1960's, and regarded by many as the most creative force in mainstream comics' history. This book is Jack Kirby's attempt to create a mythology, explaining why good triumphs over evil. The drawings may be raw, and the writing a little rough, but the book's a grenade.

Kiyama, Henry(Yoshitaka). **The Four Immigrants Manga: A Japanese Experience in San Francisco, 1904-1924.**
Stone Bridge, 1998, $12.95, ISBN 1880656337, **Y**
These poignant tales of four Japanese immigrants in San Francisco during the early part of the last century are ironic, as the immigrants attempt to understand their Caucasian employers, with humorous results. The illustrations are direct, effective, and educational. The story is framed by the years 1904-1924, as in 1924 the immigration laws stiffened, and the protagonists elected to return to Japan. This book also includes extensive notes pinpointing several of the cartoons included, as well as a biography of author/illustrator Kiyama.

Kubert, Joe. **Fax from Sarajevo.**
Dark Horse, 1996, $16.95,
ISBN 1569713464, **A**
Old comics pro Kubert writes and draws this true-to-life story from Sarajevo during the early days of the Serbian occupation, as told to him through a series of faxes, which educates the public as to the terror-filled life during that period. Kubert's artistic career serves him too well—the book at times ventures into the sentimen-

tality and sensationalism of a war comic, of the type that Kubert cut his artistic teeth on in the 1940's. Another interesting journalistic take on this subject comes from Joe Sacco's *Safe Area, Gorazde*.

Kudo, Kazuka. **Mai the Psychic Girl: The Perfect Collection.**
Viz Communications, 1995, $19.95, ISBN 156931070X, **Y**
Teenagers will enjoy the realistic, absurd, and terrifying story of Mai, who appears like most fourteen-year-olds, except for her psychic abilities. Mai thinks her powers are useful primarily for jokes, but when her father is endangered, Mai realizes that her powers are serious, and must be used with purpose.

Kuper, Peter. **The System.**
DC Comics, 1997, $12.95,
ISBN 1563893223, **A**
Taking its title from a William Blake quote, *The System* gives order to the seemingly random life of New York City. Lives intersect apparently by coincidence, in this wordless, textured drama, but in Kuper's vision there is no coincidence, only an ever-expanding connectedness. *The System's* sparse approach might turn you away, but take a deep breath and go back.

Laird, Roland, Taneshia N. Laird, & Elihu Bey. **Still I Rise: A Cartoon History of African Americans.**
Norton, 1997, $15.95, ISBN 039331751X, **Y**
This work presents American history from an African-America viewpoint, and offers nuggets of little-known information on the impact of African-Americans on American history. Though it is impossible to offer a comprehensive history in 206 pages, the Lairds and artist Elihu Bey, do a credible job of raising issues of concern to all Americans.

Lapham, David. **The Collected Stray Bullets.**
El Capitan Books, 1998, $11.95, no ISBN, **A**
They hit you when you least expect it, and your life is torn apart, those stray bullets. In this, the first volume, the characters are torn by a furious revenge, loyalty to a street boss, hatred of a step mother, thirst for political power, and sudden, unrelenting, love. The black and white illustrations are compelling and dark. For readers who want to believe that the only safety is in uncertainty.

Lee, Stan, Chris Claremont, & John Byrne. **The Dark Phoenix Saga**.
Marvel Enterainment Group, 1990, $19.95 ISBN 0939766965, **C**
Possibly the best of the X-Men graphic novels, this affecting story is executed by consumate professionals Claremont and Byrnes. Corrupting power and self sacrifice are the themes, while soul-searching Wolverine provides the pacing.

Lee, Stan & Steve Ditko. **The Essential Spider-Man.** Volume 1.
Marvel Entertainment Group, 1996, $12.99, ISBN 0785102864, **C**
Lee, Stan & Jack Kirby, et al. **The Essential Avengers.** Volume 1.
Marvel Entertainment Group, 1999, $14.95, ISBN 0785107010, **C**
Lee, Stan & Jack Kirby, et al. **The Essential Fantastic Four**. Volume 1.
Marvel Entertainment Group, 1998, $14.95, ISBN 0785106669, **C**
The "Essential" volumes reprint a score of classic comics each in black-and-white. These volumes range from the Avengers—Marvel's answer to the Justice League, featuring their greatest heroes banded together in heartfelt, entertaining tales of heroism—to the Fantastic Four—the landmark heroes that kicked off the revitalization of

the superhero genre in 1961—to Spider-Man—the defining modern hero caught between responsibility and temptation. Kirby's powerful art loses some verve without color, but Ditko's looks even better.

Lutes, Jason. **Jar of Fools**.
Black Eye, 1997, $13.99,
ISBN 0969887450, **Y**
This is the story of Ernie, a young magician who has lost his confidence, but not his magic touch. While stealing his mentor, Al Flosso, out of a nursing home, Ernie comes to terms with the tragic death of his brother. Real and insightful, this graphic novel aligns itself with literature rather than music or film.

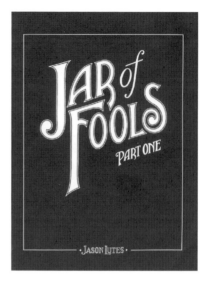

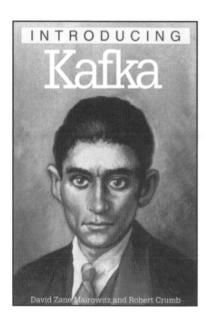

Mairowitz, David & Robert Crumb. **Introducing Kafka.**
Totem Books, 1994, $10.95,
ISBN 1874166099, **A**
Fully illustrated in black and white by Crumb, this biographical study of Kafka's life and work is incisive and compelling, and is useful to students as well as general readers interested in Kafka and the artistic process. (See also Kafka and Peter Kuper's *Give It Up!*)

McCloud, Scott. **Scott McCloud's Zot!**
Kitchen Sink Press, 1998, $19.95, ISBN 0878164294, **C**
This charming and orginal science fiction/superhero story is excellent teenage fiction that disarms the reader as it entertains. Zot and Jennie are

hesitant and revealing characters whose everyday struggle balances out the superheroic qualities of the book. The illustrations are fun and move the story along briskly.

McKean, Dave. **Cages.**
Kitchen Sink Press, 1998, $44.95, ISBN 0878166009, **A** (presently out of print, soon to be reprinted by NBM)
McKean is possibly the best known of the current artists creating work for adults, chiefly due to his prolific cover artwork in both "mature readers" comics such as Sandman and in books. Cages is the only work that McKean has written as well as drawn, and he uses the opportunity to present a dialogue on the hazards and rewards of creativity. Cages tells the story of three different artists: Leo Sabarsky, a painter in need of inspiration, Angel, a nightclub musician, who seems oblivious to to the adulation of his audience, and Jonathan Rush, whose novel Cages so enraged readers that he lives in captivity. How these characters break free of their mental cages forms the conflict of this book, which evolves into a meditation on creativity and godhood. The artwork is dynamic, and changes as McKean feels appropriate.

Miller, Frank. **300.**
Dark Horse, 2000, $30, ISBN 1569714029, **Y**
This treatment of the famous three hundred Spartan soldiers that took on the Persian Army is surprisingly well-served by Miller's hard-boiled style, honed on superhero comics and Miller's own Sin City books. An excellent use of modern genre conventions to tell a very old—and very compelling—story of bravery against impossible odds.

Miller, Frank & Klaus Janson. **Batman: The Dark Knight Returns.**
DC Comics, 1997 (reprint of 1988 edition), $14.95,
ISBN 1563893428, **Y**
Miller, Frank & David Mazzucchelli. **Batman: Year One.**
DC Comics, 1997 (reprint of 1988 edition), $9.95, ISBN 0930289331, **Y**
These two volumes, along with the 1989 feature film, led a resurgence in

popularity for this superhero icon. In Dark Knight, a fine study of vigilantes and violence, Batman at age 50 emerges from a ten-year retirement to save Gotham City from gang warfare and his nemesis, the Joker. In Year One, Miller and Mazzucchelli return to the origins of the character, and retell the first year of the life of the caped crusader after Bruce Wayne decides to don a costume and fight crime.

Moore, Alan & Steve Bissette. **The Saga of the Swamp Thing.**
DC Comics, 1987, $17.95,
ISBN 0446386901, **Y**

Wein, Len & Bernie Wrightson. **Swamp Thing: Dark Genesis.**
DC Comics, 1991, $19.95, ISBN 1563890445, **C**

The Swamp Thing comic explored what constituted humanity through the tale of biologist Alec Holland, transformed into a swamp creature by an explosion. With no hope of humanity left in his body, the Swamp Thing begins his journey back. Dark Genesis reprints the early Swamp Thing stories from the 1970's, with eerie and probing artwork from Wrightson and entertaining stories from Wein. *The Saga of the Swamp Thing* sees Moore and Bissette building on Wein and Wrightson's foundation to explore issues of the human condition in greater depth.

Moore, Alan & Brian Bolland. **Batman: The Killing Joke.**
DC Comics, 1996 (reprint of 1988 edi-

tion), $4.95, ISBN 0930289455, **Y**

The surreal and secret life of the Joker is revealed in this hypnotic tale of a promising life gone wrong. Bolland's claustrophobic illustrations give the story an eerie, otherworldly quality.

Moore, Alan & Eddie Campbell. **From Hell.**
Eddie Campbell, 1999, $35.00, ISBN 0958578346, **A**

Moore and Campbell have created a treat for horror readers, as they present this "melodrama in sixteen parts," which thoroughly investigates the Jack the Ripper murder spree in late-19th-century London. Meticulously researched and documented, *From Hell* provides atmosphere for this horrific serial murder. Campbell's scratchy drawings are riveting. This is fiction, but it is almost history. (See also Rick Geary's *Jack the Ripper*.)

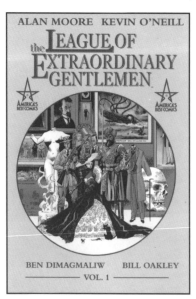

Moore, Alan, Kevin O'Neil. **The League of Extraordinary Gentlemen.**
America's Best Comics, 2000, $24.95, ISBN 1-56389-665-6, **Y**

Set in London in the waning days of the victorian era, a cast of five agents are instructed to save England. Each agent had been a respected member of society, but for various reasons—divorce, drug addiction, public shame—have drooped out of favor in the public eye. Whom they work for is uncertain; the group's leader, Miss Murray, believes it's the famed detective, Sherlock Holmes, back from the dead. Moore and O'Neil create an atmosphere that is both exciting and repressive. The script is full of wit and reference -at one point a seaman, while addressing his captain (Nemo) instructs him to "Call me Ishmael"- and the illustrations charm. Against this backdrop, creators Moore and O'Neil have superimposed a drama that is inventive and suspenseful.

Moore, Alan & Dave Gibbons.
Watchmen.
Warner Books, 1995 (reprint of 1987 edition), $20.00, ISBN 0930289234, **Y**

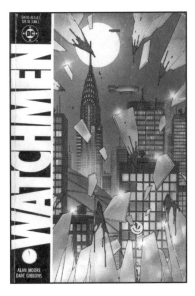

Moore and Gibbons offer what many consider to be the ultimate superhero story in the form of a meditation on time and the burdens of power. In a fantasy world, Richard Nixon never resigned after Watergate, but all the superheroes were outlawed. Those with normal (acrobatic, scientific) abilities went into hiding; Dr. Manhattan, a man atomically empowered by an explosion, was exempted, as he worked for the government. The disappearance of Dr. Manhattan brings the lesser heroes/vigilantes out of hiding, and humanity must face the result in this compelling examination of how the presence of super-powered individuals can truly change the world.

Moore, Terry. **Strangers in Paradise: I Dream of You**.
Abstract Studio, 1996, $16.95, ISBN 1892597012, **Y**
The serial *Strangers in Paradise* tells the stories of twentysomethings Katchoo, explosive and independent, and Francine, whose idea of a day well spent is returning a bird's egg to its nest. When newcomer David comes between them in this volume, there's not only jealousy and rejection in the mix, but Katchoo's dark past, which David somehow brings with him. While *Strangers in Paradise* is noteworthy for its fine character-

TERRY MOORE

STRANGERS IN PARADISE

I DREAM OF YOU

izations and human dramas, it is also a good example of how the comics medium can merge with other forms; some of the book appears as prose, and the title, "I Dream of You," is a song. A good book for those who don't read comics, an even better book for those who do. Other titles include *High School!*, *Immortal Enemies*, *It's a Good Life*, *Love Me Tender*, and *Sanctuary*.

O'Neil, Dennis & Neal Adams, et al. **Green Lantern/Green Arrow: More Hard Traveling Heroes.** DC Comics, 1993, $14.95, ISBN 1563890860, **C**

In this chapter of the Green Lantern/Green Arrow series, the heroes confront drug abuse and racism in groundbreaking stories originally published in the 1970's. Though the stories may seem dated to some, they are important parts of superhero comics history.

Outcault, R.F. **R.F. Outcault's** *The Yellow Kid***: A Centennial Celebration of the Kid Who Started the Comics.**
Kitchen Sink Press, 1995, $55.00, ISBN 0878163794, **C**
Recognized by many comic historians as the first comic strip, *The Yellow Kid* chronicles the adventures of Mickey Dugan, a poor Irish immigrant child on New York's Lower East Side. A lively introduction by comics historian Bill Blackbeard takes the reader back to turn of the century New York.

Pini, Wendy & Richard. **ElfQuest: The Hidden Years.**
Warp Graphics, 1994, $19.95, ISBN 0936861304, **Y**
In this excellent example of how the comics medium can successfully utilize fantasy themes, a race of elves search for their homeland. Other vol-

umes include the sixteen (and counting) volumes of the ElfQuest Reader's Collection series and ElfQuest: New Blood. The ElfQuest series has branched out into the prose medium as well.

Pope, Paul. **The Ballad of Doctor Richardson.**
Horse Press, 1993, $9.95,
ISBN 18242402189, **Y**
Frustrated academic Richardson asks, "Do I dare disturb the universe?" as he bumps into former student Noel on a train. The answer is yes, and Richardson's life is changed as he leaves academia, and moves into a life filled with beauty, meaning, and inspiration. Be on the lookout soon from this well-noted self-published artist for the long-awaited *THB* collection.

Porcellino, John. **Perfect Example.**
Highwater Books, 2000, $11.95, ISBN 0966536355, **Y**
This memoir presented in comics format is a quiet and ferocious piece focusing on the period between graduating from high schooland entering college. Writer/Artist Porcellino aptly depicts youthful depression and aimlessness. The spare, simple drawings illuminate and enlighten the text. Porcellino articulates the difficulties of feeling good about belonging to a peer group while not feeling good about oneself.

Schulz, Charles. **Around the World in 45 Years: Charlie Brown's Anniversary Collection.**
Andrews & McMeel, 1994, $14.95, ISBN 0836217667, **C**
Snoopy made World War I a pop culture reference, and he animated what has become the most popular newspaper strip in American history. Any of the Peanuts collections by the late Schulz will enrich your bookshelf.

Sendak, Maurice. **In the Night Kitchen.**
Harper Collins, 1995 (reprint of 1970 edition), $6.95,
ISBN 0064434362, **C**
In this ode to Mickey Mouse and Little Nemo that was awarded the
Caldecott Honor in 1971, Mickey falls out of his bed and into the night
kitchen, where he helps bakers make bread. By the book's conclusion,
readers understand why fresh bread is available every morning.

Seth. **It's a Good Life if You Don't Weaken.**
Drawn & Quarterly, 1996, $13.95, ISBN 1896597068, **A**
This bittersweet autobiographical tale tells of Seth's attempts at maturity as he drifts in and out of relationships while searching for information about "Kalo," a cartoonist who placed a piece with the New Yorker magazine in the 1950's. The pacing is meditative, and the book is kindly drawn. While readers might squirm at Seth's self-delusions, the conclusion teaches us of the redemptive power of art.

Sim, Dave. **Jaka's Story.**
Aardvark-Vanaheim, 1990, $29.95, ISBN 0919359124, **A**
This book is culled from the serial Cerebus, but Cerebus is primarily a background player. This is Jaka's story. Her husband Rick is a ne'er-do-well whom Jaka supports by working as an exotic dancer. Things go smoothly until Jaka's royal heritage is discovered, and she faces imprisonment. This is a text-heavy book,

and part of the ongoing series that also includes *Cerebus, Church and State, Church and State Volume 2, Flight, Guys, High Society, Melmoth, Reads,* and *Women.*

Smith, Jeff. **Out From Boneville.**
Cartoon Books, 1995, $19.95, ISBN 0963660993, **C**
Frequently described as one of the best –received 'family' storylines in recent years, the *BONE* books relate the poignant and entertaining misadventures of the exiled Bone family. BONE is one of the most popular books to emerge from the 1990s. If you enjoy this one, you may want to try any books in the series.

Spiegelman, Art, Francoise Mouly. **Little Lit: Folklore and Fairytale Funnies.**
HarperCollins, 2000, $19.95, ISBN 0060286245, **C**
Editors Spiegelman and Mouly have assembled some of the best of today's practitioners of the comics form in these retellings of famous and little known fairy tales. Included in this book are cartoon versions of 'Jack and the Beanstalk', 'Humpty Dumpty' as well as little known tales such as 'The Fisherman and the Sea Princess', and 'The Baker's Daughter'.

Spiegelman, Art. **Maus: A Survivor's Tale.**
Pantheon Books, 1997, $35.00, ISBN 0679406417, **Y**
This book collects both *Maus* volumes, *My Father Bleeds History* and *And Here My Troubles Began.* Volume 1 describes Spiegelman's father Vladek's struggle to survive concentration camps during World War II. Volume 2 relates the trials of Spiegelman's parents as they build a life in America. Awarded the Pulitzer prize in 1992, Maus is in part a medita-

tion on fame, success, and an exploration into familial responsibility, as Spiegelman asks what his debt is to his estranged father, and whether or not commercial success is rewarding if the price is lost autonomy. Arguably the most important piece of comic art ever published.

Steranko & Co. **Nick Fury, Agent of S.H.I.E.L.D.**
Marvel Comics, 2000, ISBN 0785107479, **Y**
This volume collects the early work of artist/writer Jim Steranko, one of the most influential creative forces of the 1960s. S.H.I.E.L.D. was Marvel's version of the F.B.I. This book primarily focuses on S.H.I.E.L.D.'s battle with HYDRA. Influences of Andy Warhol, Jack Kirby, and James Bond movies can be felt in Steranko's reaching and experimental style.

Talbot, Bryan. **The Tale of One Bad Rat.**
Dark Horse, 1995, $14.95, ISBN 1569710775, **Y**
The title of this affecting book is a nod to Beatrix Potter, whose books inspire protagonist Helen in her flight from an sexually abusive father. As she flees, Helen follows the trail of Potter in an effort to gain the strength to move on, as the abuse has ended. After a joust with the police, Helen lands a job at an inn once visited by Potter, and over time reaches the inner resolve necessary to confront her parents and take control of her life.

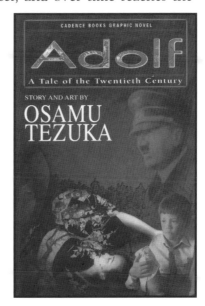

Tezuka, Osamu. **Adolf: A Tale of the Twentieth Century.**
Viz Communications, 1996, $16.95, ISBN 1569310580, **A**
Adolf is a historical novel told in five volumes, and incorporates a timeline into the narrative; this volume is the first. It is the story of three people named Adolf at the time of World War II: the infamous dictator; a half-Aryan/half-Japanese man; and a Jew living in Japan (and who is befriend-

The Tale of One Bad Rat

HOMELESS
+HUNGRY
PLEASE
HELP

by

BRYAN TALBOT

ed by the half-Aryan prior to the war). The interplay of these three Adolfs gives cartoonist Tezuka an opportunity to examine the problems of racism, facism, and personal identity. The translation is a bit rocky, and the art may be too cartoony for some readers, but this final work from the *Astro Boy* animator is the closest to an epic in comics format since Spiegelman's *Maus*. The other titles include (in order) *An Exile in Japan*, *The Half-Aryan*, *Days of Infamy*, and *1945 and All That Remains*.

Thompson, Craig. **Good-bye, Chunky Rice.**
Top Shelf Productions, 1999, $14.95, ISBN 1891830090, **Y**
Craig Thompson is a newcomer to the world of comics, but his contribution is significant. Friends Chunky Rice (a turtle) and Dandel (a mouse) appear inseparable, until Chunky Rice decides to go away, pursuing a life of surprise and adventure. In Chunky Rice's absence,

Dandel cannot be consoled. Art Spiegelman used mice to tell us about the horrors of the holocaust. Thompson uses a mouse and a turtle to instruct us in the reaches of love and loneliness, of longing and loyalty. The drawings are playful and confident, and the dialogue revealing and sure. This book has to be seen to be believed.

Tomine, Adrian, **32 Stories: The Complete *Optic Nerve* Mini-Comics.**
Drawn & Quarterly, 1998 (reprint of 1995 edition), $9.95, ISBN 1896597009, **A**
Tomine is a photographer, capturing his subjects at their most revealing. These stories turn on the glance a character makes through a window blind, upon the knowledge that one is alone in the world, and other quiet and powerful understandings. Many of the stories have an autobiographical twist. Tomine has been compared to short story writer Raymond Carver, and that's accurate up to a point, but Tomine is more surrealistic

in his conclusions.

Trudeau, G.B. **Read My Lips, Make My Day, Eat Quiche, and Die!**
Andrews & McMeel, 1989, $7.95, ISBN 0836218450, **Y**
Trudeau's protagonists Mike, Boopsie, Zonker, and J.J. play with each others' hearts and minds in this book, which also takes on career politican George Bush at the height of his administration. *Doonesbury* isn't for everybody, but, if it's to your liking, it's as American as apple pie.

Waid, Mark & Fabian Nicieza, et al. **Justice League: A Midsummer's Nightmare.**
DC Comics, 1997, $9.95, ISBN 156389338X, **C**
This collection highlights the Justice League, featuring all the flagship DC Comics heroes—Superman, Batman, Wonder Woman, Aquaman, the Flash, the Green Lantern, and the Martian Manhunter—in a well-crafted adventure that has them confront their greatest desires and fears.

Waid, Mark & Alex Ross. **Kingdom Come.**
DC Comics, 1998 (reprint of 1996 edition), $14.95,
ISBN 1563893304, **Y**
This story begins ten years after Superman has entered into a self-imposed exile. All the old heroes such as Batman and Green Lantern have either vanished or are working covertly. Superman is called back into action because the new generation of superheroes have rejected the way of life that he upholds. The resolution is unexpected and startling, and includes the birth of the next generation of heroes.

Ware, Chris. **Jimmy Corrigan: The Smartest Kid On Earth.**
Pantheon/Fantagraphics Books, 2000, $27.50, ISBN 0375404538, **A**
This book collects the "Jimmy Corrigan" stories, published piecemeal over a 7 year period. We follow protagonist Corrigan

as he learns of the existence of his absent father, watch his attempts at independence from his domineering mother, and discover his relationship with his step sister, which is strengthened as they await their father's recovery following a car accident. Ware's subtle, original dialogue between words and pictures is arresting, thought provoking, and ultimately meaningful. One does not only read Chris Ware's work, one enters it and re-emerges somehow transformed.

Watterson, Bill. **The Indispensable Calvin & Hobbes: A Calvin & Hobbes Treasury.**
Andrews & McMeel, 1992, $12.95, ISBN 0836218981 C
Any Calvin & Hobbes collection is worth a look, as it was the freshest newspaper strip in many years. With consumate skill, Watterson told the insightful tale of hyperactive six-year-old protagonist Calvin, and Hobbes, his stuffed tiger, who is the major participant in his world.
Other especially recommended titles include *The Authoritative Calvin & Hobbes, Calvin & Hobbes: Tenth Anniversary,* and *The Essential Calvin & Hobbes.*

Wilde, Oscar & P. Craig Russell. **The Fairy Tales of Oscar Wilde: The Birthday of the Infanta.**
NBM, 1998, $15.95, ISBN 1561632139, C
This is one of a series of adaptations of Wilde's stories, which is handsomely presented and preserves the mythic quality of the tales by utilizing a colorful cartoon format. Other titles include *The Selfish Giant* and *the Star Child* and *The Young King* and *Remarkable Rocket.*

Wolfman, Marv, Perez, George. **Crisis on Infinite Earths**
DC Comics, 2001, $29.95, ISBN 1563897504, C

This volume collects the series first released by DC in the mid 1980s. Its attempt to re-organize and streamline the multiple characters in the DC universe was, in great part, successful, and features a great majority of the characters DC has made popular over the years. Reads better as a collected work than as a series of consecutive issues.

Woodring, Jim. Frank. **Volume 1.**
Fantagraphics Books, 1998, $16.95, ISBN 01560971533, **A**
These wordless stories featuring a cat named Frank are dreams, nightmares, and visions. Children will enjoy them, teenagers will identify with them, and adults will understand them. Also available is *Frank* Volume 2.

Yeh, Phil. **Winged Tiger's World Peace Party Puzzle Book.**
Hawaya Inc., 1997 (reprint of 1993 edition), $11.95,
ISBN 0964414910, **C**
Children will be fascinated by this purely visual story of an elusive, intrusive world-traveling flying cat. Influences of Chaplin can be felt in these pages, which hold no narration nor word balloons.

Novels Featuring
Comic Book
Characters

Novels, and other prose pieces featuring comic book characters, first emerged in the late 1960s, with two novels featuring characters appearing in Marvel Comics. In the late 1980s, DC Comics released a line of comic book character novels, but these were not well received. In the 1990s, Byron Preiss Multimedia and Berkley Boulevard Books released a prominent series of novels featuring characters from Marvel Comics. Novels featuring characters who are not Marvel or DC are far and few between. Occasionally, a "serious" novel featuring comic book characters will appear (one example is Jay Cantor's *Krazy Kat*, Knopf, 1988) but primarily books featuring comic book characters are aimed at the same readers who enjoy comics themselves, but are also receptive to stories of these characters in prose format.

There are advantages to the prose novel featuring comic book characters. The form may introduce readers who may be unfamiliar with certain characters, or uncomfortable with the comics format, to a new setting in which to experience these characters. Another advantage of the novel format is that it allows the writers an opportunity to explore aspects of the characters which may not be prominent within the comic book series. Finally, novels featuring comic book characters allow a greater depth of characterization than is generally found in serialized issues.

Novels featuring comic book characters may lead people to the comics themselves, as well as to other reading experiences. In this section, I have noted several prose books featuring comic book characters. This is a very short list, but its attempt is to be representational of the genre.

Gaiman, Neil. **The Sandman: The Dream Hunters.**
DC Comics, 1999, $29.95, ISBN 1563895730
Gaiman successfully weaves the Sandman characters into this re-telling of the Japanese folktale, "The Fox, the Monk, and the Mikado of All Night's Dreaming," and overcomes the difficulty of remaining true to the original folk tale while placing the story tangientally within the boundaries of his *Sandman* series. Illustrated in brush and ink by Yoshitaka Amano in a style reminiscent of classic Japanese art.

Gardner, Craig Shaw. **Spider-Man: Wanted Dead or Alive.**
Berkley Boulevard, 1999 (reprint of 1998 edition), $6.99, ISBN 0425169308

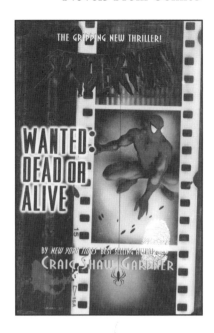

Veteran fantasist Gardner tells this story laced with humor reminiscent of the original Lee/Ditko Amazing Spider-Man series, in which Spider-Man is plagued by a public that doubts his altruistic motives, and finds himself blamed first for the shooting of an innocent bystander, then in the murder of a prominent political figure. Spider-Man does clear his name, but in doing so, has to battle arch-enemies Electro and the Rhino, all the while trying to break the crime syndicate behind the frame-up. With evocative black-and-white illustrations by Bob Hall.

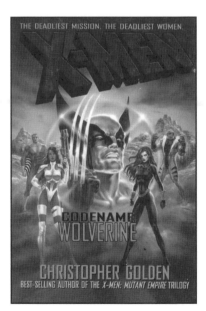

Golden, Christopher. **X-Men: Codename Wolverine.**
Berkley Boulevard, 2000 (reprint of 1998 edition), $6.99, ISBN 0425171116

In this engrossing espionage thriller that spans both a prior mission and a present danger, Wolverine—the most popular member of the X-Men superhero team—is captured as a result of a mission he accomplished in years past. He and a group of fellow heroes and villians, the Black Widow, Sabretooth, Banshee, Mystique, and Wraith, are forced to come to terms with a murder committed while on a government mission. At the novel's conclusion, not only has Wolverine realized how his code of ethics has changed since joining the

X-Men, but that he may not forgive a past that he genuinely regrets.

Lee, Stan, Editor. **The Ultimate Silver Surfer.**
Berkley Boulevard, 1997 (reprint of 1995 edition), $6.50, ISBN 1572972998
This short-story collection features stories of Norrin Radd, also known as the Silver Surfer, one of the more tragic yet noble heroes in the Marvel Comics universe. Various writers from the science fiction, fantasy, and comic book fields tell new stories of the Silver Surfer's heroism. Illustrated by various artists.

O'Neil, Dennis. **Batman: Knightfall.**
Bantam Books, 1995 (reprint of 1994 edition), $5.99, ISBN 0553572601
Denny O'Neil is group editor of the Batman comics, and is responsible for some of the most memorable Batman stories over the last thirty years. This is a novelization of a storyline first serialized in the various Batman comics, in which Batman's enemy Bane releases the inmates of Arkham Asylum. As Batman fights both his enemies and serious injury, he must confront his own future as well as the future role of Batman.

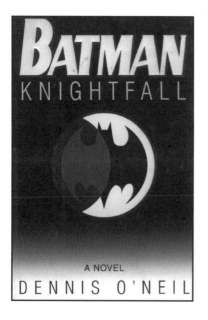

Pini, Richard & Wendy. **ElfQuest: Journey to Sorrow's End.**
Ace Books, 1993, $5.99, ISBN 0441183719
ElfQuest is the continuing story of a group of elves in search of their home-

land. This installment, an adaptation from the comic book series, tells the story of the tragic love triangle of Cutter, the Wolf Rider; Leetah, the Healer; and Rayak of the Sun Folk. Written by the Pinis, who created the series, this book also contains character histories not found in the comic book.

Further Reading

about and related
to Comics

ARTICLES

•Beahm, George, "Graphic Novels: Comics, Magazines, or Books?" *Publishers Weekly*, November 6, 1987, p. 22.

•Bruggeman, Laura, "ZAP! WHOOSH! KERPLOW!: Build High-Quality Graphic Novel Collections with Impact," *School Library Journal*, January, 1997, p. 22.

•Cocks, Jay, "The Passing of POW! and BLAM!: Comics Grow Up, Get Ambitious, and Turn Into Graphic Novels," *Time*, January 25, 1988, p. 65.

•Dardess, George, "Understanding Comics," *College English*, February, 1995, p. 213.

•DeCandido, Keith R.A., "Picture This: Graphic Novels in Libraries," Library Journal, March 15, 1990, p. 50.

•Gagnier, Richard S., "A Hunger for Heroes: Comics Feed a Need for Heroism at an Unstable Time of Life," School *Library Journal*, September, 1997 p. 143.

•Pederson, Martin, "Comics at 100: Still Growing," *Publisher's Weekly*, June 12, 1995, p. 32.

•Reid, Calvin, "Comics: A User's Guide," *Publishers Weekly*, October 11, 1993, p. 54.

•"Tintin and the Intellectuals," *The Economist*, June 29, 1996, p. 86.

•Weiner, Stephen, "Creating a Graphic Novel Collection for the Public Library," *Voice of Youth Advocates*, December, 1992, p. 69.

BOOKS

Crumb, Robert. **Your Vigor for Life Appalls Me: Robert Crumb Letters 1958-1977.**
Fantagraphics Books, 1998, $14.95, ISBN 1560973102
In these letters, underground comix master Crumb reveals his search for meaning through thought, art, and sex. Includes some black and white illustrations in the form of letters.

Daniels, Les. **Marvel: Five Fabulous Decades of the World's Greatest Comics.**
Abrams, 1991, $35.00, ISBN 0810938219.
This single volume offers a concise and critical history of Marvel's rise to the forefront of the world of commercial comic book publishing. Includes biographical information on comic book creators as well as Marvel's famed characters.
Daniels has also written three similarly-themed volumes on the "big three" of DC Comics superhero-dom: *Batman, the Complete History: The Life and Times of the Dark Knight, Superman, the Complete History: The Golden Age of America's First Hero, and Wonder Woman, the Complete History: The Life and Times of the Amazon Princess.*

Dorfman, Ariel & Arman Mattehart. **How to Read Donald Duck: Imperialist Ideology in the Disney Comic.** 2nd ed.
International General, 1991 (reprint of 1984 edition), $12.95, ISBN 0884770230.
This study of imperialism in the Disney comic remains critical in the twenty-five years since its first publication. Comics are a primary vehicle

for popular culture, and in this invaluable work, authors Dorfman and Mattehart study the dangers of pop culture, specifically its impact on the Third World.

Eisner, Will. **Comics and Sequential Art.**
Poorhouse Press, 1985, $14.95, ISBN 0961742802.
Comics grandmaster Eisner draws upon a career of creating and packaging comics and graphic novels, as well as a career as adjunct faculty at the School of Visual Arts, as he explains and demonstrates how sequential art is produced and why its effect is so powerful. Fully illustrated in black and white. The author includes numerous historical and international examples.

Hogarth, Burne. **Dynamic Figure Drawing**.
Watson-Guptill, $19.95, ISBN 0823015777.
This classic by the grand master of the Tarzan Sunday comic strips may be the *sine qua non* for aspiring comics artists. While a regular art instruction book, its emphasis on the portrayal of movement makes it essential for learning the art of comics. Watson-Guptill still has available a number of other such titles by Hogarth.

Horn, Maurice. **The World Encyclopedia of Comics.**
Chelsea House, 1999,. $35.00, ISBN 0791048543.
This update of the Horn classic from 1976 details characters, creators, and comics

issues internationally. A vital addition to any comics library.

Jones, Gerard & Will Jacobs. **The Comic Book Heroes.**
Prima Publishing, 1997, $19.95, ISBN 0761503935
Jones and Jacobs ably offer an history of the comics industry since the 1960s. Filled with insightful and up-to-date information, readers are given an overview of the field and clarity as to many of the challenges the industry faces. This book is a good companion to the excellent out-of-print history *The Steranko History of Comics* by Jim Steranko (Supergraphics, 1970).

McCloud, Scott.
Understanding Comics.
HarperPerennial, 1994, $22.50, ISBN 006097625X

McCloud's study is both a treatise on how comics work and a history of the medium. It's unique in the sense that it uses the comics medium to talk about itself, thus giving those evaluating and discussing the medium a common language. This is one of the best received books using comic format outside of the primarily comics' readership, and is a necessary volume on the language of the medium. Also recommended is McCloud's follow-up volume, *Reinventing Comics*.

Robbins, Trina. **From Girls to Grrrlz: a History of Women's Comics from Teens to Zines.**
Chronicle, 1999, $17.95, ISBN 0811821994.
Unlocking a previously barred closet in comic book history, this book focuses on comic strips and comic books created, written, and drawn by women with abundant illustrations.

BOOKS ON COMICS AND GRAPHIC NOVELS THAT ARE OUT OF PRINT,
but essential. Find them in your library!

Drooker, Eric. **Flood!**
Four Walls, Eight Windows, 1992.
Flood! is Drooker's haunting tale of a life on the brink of collapse. An artist is laid off and has a brief, surrealistic affair with a junkie, and then returns to his loft to create the haunting book *Flood!*, the volume that the reader holds. Both the interior book and the physical one are hypnotic, compelling, and terrifying. Drooker's story is told wordlessly, and his woodblock illustrations pay homage to Lynd Ward and Robert Crumb as they tell this chilling tale of urban survival. *Flood!* was short-

listed for the 1992 National Book Award. (Readers may also want to try Ward's *Storyteller Without Words: The Wood Engravings of Lynd Ward*, Abrams, 1974.)

Feiffer, Jules. **The Great Comic Book Heroes.**
Dial Press, 1965.
Feiffer offers insightful commentary on the comic book industry prior to World War II. Perhaps his argument as to why pop culture is so powerful remains the most important contribution of the book. Includes early adventures of premier heroes such as Batman and the Human Torch. Check your library for this one. (Text essay reproduced in full in *The Comics Journal #200*.)

Herriman, George. **The Komplete Kolor Krazy Kat.**
World Service Books, 1993.

Regarded by many as the greatest newspaper strip in the history of American comics, Krazy Kat is reproduced here in full color. The physical and obsessive humor is evident, and evocations of America's innocence are present in the characters of the innocent Krazy Kat, the cruel Ignatz Mouse, and the beleaguered Offissa Pup. Krazy Kat et al are the protagonists of a serious novel of the same name by Jay Cantor.

Miller, Frank & David Mazzucchelli. **Daredevil: Born Again.**
Marvel Entertainment Group, 1990,
Miller and Mazzucchelli tell this story of Daredevil, a blind, acrobatic hero, who sees by using a radioactive "radar" sense. Daredevil's enemy, the Kingpin, learns his secret identity, and uses the information to destroy him. The loss teaches Daredevil at once how important and how irrelevant his secret identity is to him.

Steranko, James. **The Steranko History of Comics.**
Supergraphics, 1970. Two volumes.
This double-volume history describes the evolution of comic (book) magazines from earlier popular "pulp" magazines. The second volume describes the creation of the early major superhero characters, covering the period between 1908-1950. Lavishly illustrated, primarily with pulp and comic book magazine covers.

Witek, Joseph. **Comic Books as History: The Narrative Art of Jack Jackson, Art Spiegelman, and Harvey Pekar.**
University of Mississippi Press, 1990.
Witek uses critical methodology as he examines the work of current comic artists from a critical perspective. This is a particularly useful work as it includes a lengthy study of Spiegelman's Maus.

Index
by title

A

Adolf: A Tale of the Twentieth Century. Tezuka, Osamu. Viz Communications, 1996, 51
Around the World in 45 Years: Charlie Brown's Anniversary Collection. Schulz, Charles. Andrews & McMeel, 1994, 48
Aviation Art of Russell Keaton, The. Keaton, Russell. Kitchen Sink Press, 1995, 36

B

Ballad of Doctor Richardson, The. Pope, Paul. Horse Press, 1993, 48
Batman: Knightfall. O'Neil, Dennis. Bantam Books, 1995 (reprint of 1994 edition), 64
Batman: The Dark Knight Returns. Miller, Frank & Klaus Janson. DC Comics, 1997(reprint of 1988 edition), 42
Batman: The Killing Joke. Moore, Alan & Brian Bolland. DC Comics, 1996 (reprint of 1988 edition), 43
Batman: Year One. Miller, Frank & David Mazzucchelli. DC Comics, 1997 (reprint of 1988 edition), 42
Big Baby. Burns, Charles. Fantagraphics Books, 1999, 22
Books of Magic, The. Gaiman, Neil, et al. DC Comics, 1993, 29
Borden Tragedy, The : A Memoir of the Infamous Double Murder at Fall River, Mass., 1892. Geary, Rick. NBM, 1997, 30

C

Cages. McKean, Dave. Kitchen Sink Press, 1998, 42
Chandler's Philip Marlowe. Fireside Books, 1997, 24
Classic Star Wars. Goodwin, Archie & Al Williamson. Dark Horse, 1995 (reprint of 1990 edition), 33
Collected Stray Bullets, The. Lapham, David. El Capitan Books, 1998, 40
Comic Book Heroes, The. Jones, Gerard & Will Jacobs. Prima Publishing, 1997, 72

Comic Books as History: The Narrative Art of Jack Jackson, Art Spiegelman, and Harvey Pekar. Witek, Joseph. University of Mississippi Press, 1990, 74

Comics and Sequential Art. Eisner, Will. Poorhouse Press, 1985, 71

Complete Crumb Comics, The : The Death of Fritz the Cat. Crumb, Robert. Fantagraphics Books, 1992, 25

Contract with God and Other Tenement Stories, A. Eisner, Will. DC Comics, 2000 (reprint of 1978 edition), 26

Crisis on Infinite Earths. Wolfman, Marv, Perez, George. DC Comics, 2001, 56

D

Daredevil: Born Again. Miller, Frank & David Mazzucchelli. Marvel Entertainment Group, 1990, 74

Dark Phoenix Saga, The. Lee, Stan, Chris Claremont, & John Byrne. Marvel Entertainment Group, 1990, 40

Dykes to Watch Out For. Bechdel, Alison. Firebrand Books, 1995, 20

Dynamic Figure Drawing. Hogarth, Burne. Watson-Guptill, 71

E

ElfQuest: Journey to Sorrow's End. Pini, Richard & Wendy. Ace Books, 1993, 64

ElfQuest: The Hidden Years. Pini, Wendy & Richard. Warp Graphics, 1994, 47

Essential Avengers, The. Volume 1. Lee, Stan & Jack Kirby, et al. Marvel Entertainment Group, 1999, 40

Essential Fantastic Four, The. Volume 1. Lee, Stan & Jack Kirby, et al. Marvel Entertainment Group, 1998, 40

Essential Spider-Man, The. Volume 1. Lee, Stan & Steve Ditko. Marvel Entertainment Group, 1996, 40

Ethel & Ernest. Briggs, Raymond. Jonathan Cape, 1998, 21

F

Fairy Tales of Oscar Wilde, The : The Birthday of the Infanta. Wilde, Oscar & P. Craig Russell. NBM, 1998, 56

Fax from Sarajevo. Kubert, Joe. Dark Horse, 1996, 38

Flood! Drooker, Eric. Four Walls, Eight Windows, 1992, 73

Fortune and Glory. Bendis, Brian Michael. Oni Press, 2000, 21

Four Immigrants Manga, The : A Japanese Experience in San Francisco, 1904-1924. Kiyama, Henry(Yoshitaka). Stone Bridge, Distributed by Consortium, 1998, 38

From Girls to Grrrlz: a History of Women's Comics from Teens to Zines. Robbins, Trina. Chronicle, 1999, 72

From Hell. Moore, Alan & Eddie Campbell. Eddie Campbell, 1999, 44

G

Ghostworld. Clowes, Daniel. Fantagraphic Books, 1997, 25

Give It Up! and Other Stories by Franz Kafka. Kafka, Franz & Peter Kuper. NBM, 1995, 35

Good-bye, Chunky Rice. Thompson, Craig. Top Shelf Productions, 1999, 53

Great Comic Book Heroes, The. Feiffer, Jules. Dial Press, 1965, 73

Greatest Joker Stories Ever Told, The. DC Comics, 1989, 33

Greatest Superman Stories Ever Told, The. DC Comics, 1987, 33

Greatest Team-Up Stories Ever Told, The. DC Comics, 1991, 33

Green Lantern/Green Arrow: More Hard Traveling Heroes. O'Neil, Dennis & Neal Adams, et al. DC Comics, 1993, 47

Groo & Rufferto. Aragones, Sergio & Mark Evanier. Dark Horse, 2000, 19

H

Hey Buddy! Volume 1 of the Complete Buddy Bradley Stories from *Hate*. Bagge, Peter. Fantagraphics Books, 1995, 19

How to Read Donald Duck: Imperialist Ideology in the Disney Comic. 2nd ed. Dorfman, Ariel & Arman Mattehart. International General, 1991 (reprint of 1984 edition), 70

I

I Never Liked You. Brown, Chester. Drawn & Quarterly, 1994, 22

In the Night Kitchen. Sendak, Maurice. HarperCollins, 1995 (reprint of 1970 edition), 49

Indispensable Calvin & Hobbes, The : A Calvin & Hobbes Treasury. Watterson, Bill. Andrews & McMeel, 1992, 56

Introducing Kafka. Mairowitz, David & Robert Crumb. Totem Books, 1994, 41

It's a Good Life if You Don't Weaken. Seth. Drawn & Quarterly, 1996, 49

J

Jack Kirby's New Gods. Kirby, Jack. DC Comics, 1998, 38

Jack the Ripper: A Journal of the Whitechapel Murders 1888-1889. Geary, Rick. NBM, 1995, 31

Jaka's Story. Sim, Dave. Aardvark-Vanaheim, 1990, 49

Jar of Fools. Lutes, Jason. Black Eye, 1997, 41

Jew in Communist Prague, A, Vol.1: Loss of Innocence. Giardino, Vittorio. NBM ComicsLit, 1997, 31

Jimmy Corrigan: The Smartest Kid On Earth. Ware, Chris. Pantheon/Fantagraphics Books, 2000, 54

Judas Contract, The. Wolfman, Marv & George Pérez. DC Comics, 1989, 57

Julius Knipl, Real Estate Photographer: Stories. Katchor, Ben. Little Brown, 1996, 36

Justice League: A Midsummer's Nightmare. Waid, Mark & Fabian Nicieza, et al. DC Comics, 1997, 54

K

Kingdom Come. Waid, Mark & Alex Ross. DC Comics, 1998 (reprint of 1996 edition), 54

Komplete Kolor Krazy Kat, The. Herriman, George. World Service Books, 1993, 73

Kurt Busiek's Astro City: Life in the Big City. Busiek, Kurt & Brent Anderson. DC Comics, 2000 (reprint of 1996 edition), 22

L

Larry Gonick's The Cartoon History of the Universe. Gonick, Larry. William Morrow, 1982, 33

League of Extraordinary Gentlemen, The. Moore, Alan, Kevin O'Neil. America's Best Comics, 2000, 44

Little Lit: Folklore and Fairytale Funnies. Spiegelman, Art, Mouly, Francoise. HarperCollins, 2000, 50

Look Inside For Better or For Worse, A : The Tenth Anniversary Collection. Johnston, Lynn. Andrews & McMeel, 1989, 35

Lost Cause: The True Story of Famed Texas Gunslinger John Wesley Hardin. Jackson, Jack. Kitchen Sink Press, 1998, 35

Lost Girl. Kanan, Nabiel. NBM, 1999, 36

Love & Rockets: Poison River. Hernandez, Gilbert. Fantagraphics Books, 1994, 34

M

Madman: The Oddity Odyssey. Allred, Michael. Acacia Press, 1999, 19

Mai the Psychic Girl: The Perfect Collection. Kudo, Kazuka. Viz Communications, 1995, 39

Man of Steel. Byrne, John. DC Comics, 1988, 24

Marvel: Five Fabulous Decades of the World's Greatest Comics. Daniels, Les. Abrams, 1991, 70

Marvels. Busiek, Kurt & Alex Ross. Marvel Entertainment Group, 1994, 24

Maus: A Survivor's Tale. Spiegelman, Art. Pantheon Books, 1997, 50

*Meanwhile...*Feiffer, Jules. HarperCollins, 1999 (reprint of 1997 edition, 28

Minor Miracles. Eisner, Will. DC Comics, 2000, 26

Mr. Punch. Gaiman, Neil & Dave McKean. DC Comics, 1994, 30

N

Nick Fury, Agent of S.H.I.E.L.D. Steranko & Co. Marvel Comics, 2000, 51

O

Our Cancer Year. Brabner, Joyce, Harvey Pekar & Frank Stack. Four Walls, Eight Windows, 1994, 21

Out From Boneville. Smith, Jeff. Cartoon Books, 1995, 50

Outcault's The Yellow Kid: A Centennial Celebration of the Kid Who Started the Comics. Outcault, R.F. Kitchen Sink Press, 1995, 47

P

Perfect Example. Porcellino, John. Highwater Books, 2000, 48
Pogo. Volume 11. Kelly, Walt. Fantagraphics Books, 2000, 37

Q

Queen of the Black Black. Kelso, Megan. Highwater Books, 1998, 37

R

Raymond Chandler's Philip Marlowe: My Little Sister. Chandler, Raymond & Michael Lark. Fireside Books, 1997, 24
Read My Lips, Make My Day, Eat Quiche, and Die! Trudeau, G.B. Andrews & McMeel, 54
Rudyard Kipling's Jungle Book. Kipling, Rudyard & P. Craig Russell. NBM, 1997, 37

S

Saga of the Swamp Thing, The. Moore, Alan & Steve Bissette. DC Comics, 1987, 43
Sandman, The : The Doll's House. Gaiman, Neil, et al. DC Comics, 1990, 29
Sandman, The : The Dream Hunters. Gaiman, Neil. DC Comics, 1999, 61
Scott McCloud's Zot! McCloud, Scott. Kitchen Sink Press, 1998, 41
Simpsons Comics a Go-Go. Groening, Matt, et al. HarperPerennial, 2000, 34
Snowman, The. Briggs, Raymond. Random House, 1995 (reprint of 1978 edition), 21
Spider-Man: Wanted Dead or Alive. Gardner, Craig Shaw. Berkley Boulevard, 1999 (reprint of 1998 edition), 63
Spirit Archives, The. Eisner, Will. DC Comics, 2000, 28
Star Trek: The Modala Imperative. Friedman, Michael Jan, Peter David, & Pablo Marcos. DC Comics, 1992, 29
Steranko History of Comics, The. Steranko, James. Supergraphics, 1970, 74
Still I Rise: A Cartoon History of African Americans. Laird, Roland, Taneshia N. Laird, & Elihu Bey. Norton, 1997, 39
Strangers in Paradise: I Dream of You. Moore, Terry. Abstract Studio, 1996, 45
Stuck Rubber Baby. Cruse, Howard. DC Comics, 1995, 25
Swamp Thing: Dark Genesis. Wein, Len & Bernie Wrightson. DC Comics, 1991, 43
System, The. Kuper, Peter. DC Comics, 1997, 39

T

Tale of One Bad Rat, The. Talbot, Bryan. Dark Horse, 1995, 51
Tantrum! Feiffer, Jules. Fantagraphics Books, 1997 (reprint of 1979 edition), 28
32 Stories: The Complete Optic Nerve Mini-Comics. Tomine, Adrian. Drawn & Quarterly,

1998 (reprint of 1995 edition), 53
300. Miller, Frank. Dark Horse, 2000, 42
Tintin in Tibet. Hergé. Little, Brown, 1988 (reprint of 1975 edition), 34
To The Heart of The Storm. Eisner, Will. DC Comics, 2000, 26

U

Ultimate Silver Surfer, The. Lee, Stan, Editor. Berkley Boulevard, 1997 (reprint of 1995 edition), 64
Understanding Comics. McCloud, Scott. HarperPerennial, 1994, 72

V

Violent Cases. Gaiman, Neil & Dave McKean. Kitchen Sink Press, 1998, (reprint of 1987 edition), 30

W

Watchmen. Moore, Alan & Dave Gibbons. Warner Books, 1995 (reprint of 1987 edition), 45
Why I Hate Saturn. Baker, Kyle.DC Comics, 1998 (reprint of 1990 edition), 20
Winged Tiger's World Peace Party Puzzle Book. Yeh, Phil. Hawaya Inc., 1997 (reprint of 1993 edition), 57
World Encyclopedia of Comics, The. Horn, Maurice. Chelsea House, 1999, 71

X

X-Men: Codename Wolverine. Golden, Christopher. Berkley Boulevard, 2000 (reprint of 1998 edition), 63

Y

Your Vigor for Life Appalls Me: Robert Crumb Letters 1958-1977. Crumb, Robert. Fantagraphics Books, 1998, 70

Z

Zippy Annual #1. Griffith, Bill. Fantagraphic Books, 2000, 33